Emily Davies

The Higher Education of Women

Emily Davies

The Higher Education of Women

ISBN/EAN: 9783744771740

Printed in Europe, USA, Canada, Australia, Japan

Cover: Foto ©Andreas Hilbeck / pixelio.de

More available books at **www.hansebooks.com**

THE HIGHER EDUCATION

OF WOMEN

ALEXANDER STRAHAN, PUBLISHER

LONDON,   .   148 *Strand*

NEW YORK.   .   .   .   178 *Grand Street*

THE HIGHER EDUCATION

OF WOMEN

BY EMILY DAVIES

Anchora Spei

ALEXANDER STRAHAN, PUBLISHER

LONDON AND NEW YORK

1866

CONTENTS.

CHAPTER I.

INTRODUCTORY.

IN any inquiry of a practical nature, intended to lead to some definite course of action, it is obviously necessary to start with a tolerably clear idea of the end in view—the object for which it is proposed to provide. In the case of education, definitions more or less satisfactory have already so often been given, that it might seem superfluous to go into the question again. As a matter of practice, however, it is found that, when it is attempted to apply the received definitions of the general objects of education to the case of women, they are usually questioned or modified, if not altogether set aside. When, for instance, Mr Maurice tells us that 'the end of education itself is, as it has always been considered, to form a nation of living, orderly men,' the definition will be accepted, with the tacit reservation that it applies only to men, in the exclusive sense of the word, and has nothing to do with the education of women. Again, when Milton, in his treatise on Education, lays down that the end of learning is 'to repair the ruin of our first parents by regaining to know God aright, and out of that knowledge to love Him, to imitate Him, to be like Him,' the language might be taken in a general sense ; and when he goes on to define a complete and generous education as 'that which fits a man to perform justly, skilfully, and magnanimously all the offices, both private and public, of peace and war,' the words might still, perhaps, bear a common interpretation ; but as soon as he comes to describing in detail, 'how all this may be done between twelve and one-and-twenty,' it becomes evident that he is thinking of boys only. In the most recent writers, the tendency to regard general theories of education as applying exclusively to that of men, is quite as strongly marked.

It seems, therefore, that in attempting to treat of female education, it is necessary once more to ask what we are aiming at, and to obtain, if possible, a clear understanding and agreement as to the end in view. What ought the educators of girls to be trying to make of them? What is the ideal towards which they ought to direct their efforts, the end to be desired as the result of their labours?

To these questions we shall probably receive one or other of two answers. Many persons will reply, without hesitation, that the one object to be aimed at, the ideal to be striven after, in the education of women, is to make good wives and mothers. And the answer is a reasonable one, so far as it goes, and with explanations. Clearly, no education would be good which did not tend to make good wives and mothers; and that which produces the best wives and mothers is likely to be the best possible education. But, having made this admission, it is necessary to point out that an education of which the aim is thus limited, is likely to fail in that aim. That this is so will appear when the definition is transferred to the education of men. It will be admitted that a system of education which should produce bad husbands and fathers would prove itself to be bad; and an education which produces the best husbands and fathers is likely to be in all

respects the best; because the best man
in any capacity must be the man who
can measure most accurately the proportion of all his duties and claims, giving
to each its due share of his time and
energy. A man will not be the better
husband and father for neglecting his
obligations as a citizen, or as a man of
business. Nor will a woman be the
better wife or mother through ignorance
or disregard of other responsibilities.
There is, indeed, a view of male education which, having worldly advancement
for its ultimate object, regards it exclusively as a means of acquiring professional dexterity; but such a conception
of the purposes of education—however
legitimate, in a limited and subordinate

sense — when elevated into the position of the final goal, must be looked upon rather as a lapse from a higher standard, than as a principle deliberately maintained by any high-minded and thoughtful person. In disinterested schemes of male education, it is usually assumed, as a matter of course, that the great object is to make the best of a man in every respect, leaving him to adapt himself to specific relations, according to the state of life into which it shall .please God to call him.

A similar idea seems to underlie the other, and more comprehensive reply, which will probably be given to our inquiry, namely, that the object of female education is to produce women of the best and highest type, not limited by exclusive regard to any specific functions hereafter to be discharged by them. This answer at once brings down upon us the terrible question, What *is* the best and highest type of woman? And as this question lies at the root of the whole matter, it cannot be passed by. Many people, indeed, talk as if it was a matter on which the world had long since made up its mind, and which might be assumed to be already decided. But when we ask what it is that the world has decided, it is difficult to obtain anything like a clear and unanimous answer. The ideal differs not only among different races, and in different ages, but most widely in our own country, and in modern times. Unanimity is scarcely to be found in any class of writers or thinkers, though on this point, of all others, some sort of agreement, at least between parents and teachers, would seem to be most essential. It may perhaps be of service, as a step towards a mutual understanding, to examine, though necessarily in a very imperfect and cursory manner, some of the most commonly received notions current on the subject.

CHAPTER II.

IDEALS.

THERE is a theory afloat, extensively prevalent, and probably influencing many persons who have never stated it definitely to themselves, that the human ideal is composed of two elements, the male and the female, each requiring the other as its complement; and that the realisation of this ideal is to be found in no single human

being, man or woman, but in the union
of individuals by marriage, or by some
sort of vague marriage of the whole race.
The conception of character which rests
on the broad basis of a common human-
ity falls into the background, and there
is substituted for it a dual theory, with
distinctly different forms of male and
female excellence. Persons who take
this view are naturally governed by
it in their conceptions of what women
ought to be. Having framed a more
or less definite idea of the masculine
character, in constructing the feminine
helpmeet they look out, if not for the
directly opposite, for what they would
call the complementary qualities, and the
conclusion quickly follows, that whatever

B

is manly must be unwomanly, and *vice versâ*. The advocates of this view usually hold in connexion with it certain doctrines, such as, that the man is intended for the world, woman for the home; man's strength is in the head, woman's in the heart; the man's function is to protect, woman's to soothe and comfort; men must work, and women must weep: everywhere we are to have a sharply marked division, often honestly mistaken for the highest and most real communion. Closely connected with these separatist doctrines is the double moral code, with its masculine and feminine virtues, and its separate law of duty and honour for either sex.

The general acceptance of the theory

is not surprising. It gratifies the logical instinct; and many persons, hastily taking for granted that it is the only conception of the relations between men and women which recognises real distinctions, assume it to be the only one which satisfies the craving of the æsthetic sense for harmony and fitness. Unfortunately it is not workable. We make the world even more puzzling than it is by nature, when we shut our eyes to the facts of daily life; and we know, as a fact, that women have a part in the world, and that men are by no means ciphers in the home circle—we know that a man who should be all head would be as monstrous an anomaly as a woman all heart—that men require the protection of law, and women are not so uniformly prosperous as to be independent of comfort and consolation—men have no monopoly of working, nor women of weeping. The sort of distinction it is attempted to establish, though not without an element of truth when rightly understood, is for the most part artificial, plausible in appearance, but breaking down under the test of experience. When overstrained, and made the foundation of a divided moral code, it is misleading in proportion to its attractiveness.

Happily this theory, though deeply and widely and most subtilely influential, is not completely dominant. People who go to church, and who read their Bibles, are perpetually reminded of one type and exemplar, one moral law. The theory of education of our English Church recognises no distinction of sex. The baptized child is signed with the sign of the cross, 'in token that hereafter he—or she—shall not be ashamed to confess the faith of Christ crucified, and manfully to fight under His banner, against sin, the world, and the devil; and to continue Christ's faithful soldier and servant to his—or her—life's end.' The sponsors are charged to provide that the child be 'virtuously brought up to lead a godly and a Christian life, remembering always that baptism doth represent unto us our profession, which is to follow the example of our Saviour Christ, and to be made like unto Him.' The catechism in which the child is to be

like, or we may want what will do us
good — and the two qualities are not
always combined.   Usually, however, it
is taken for granted that, in this case,
men like what is good for them ; and it
only remains, therefore, to be ascertained
what it is that they like.

There is no lack of evidence.   English
literature is full of oracular information
on the subject.   Mr Anthony Trollope
says :   'We like women to be timid.'
Mr Helps complains that ' women are
not taught to be courageous.   Indeed, to
some persons courage may seem as un-
necessary for women as Latin and Greek.
Yet there are few things that would tend
to make women happier in themselves,
and more acceptable to those with whom

they live, than courage. . . . So far from courage being unfeminine, there is a peculiar grace and dignity in those beings who have little active power of attack or defence, passing through danger with a moral courage which is equal to that of the strongest.'

Abundance of applause has been bestowed upon Miss Nightingale and the other 'heroines of the Crimea,' whose enterprise certainly required no small share of masculine resolution. On the other hand, a writer on the position of women confesses to 'an admiration for the commonplace, unambitious kind of old maid, who is content to do good in her own neighbourhood, and among the few persons whom she really knows—who takes a lively interest in the welfare of her nephews and nieces, and who regales herself occasionally with tea and gossip.'

One writer tells us that there are things for which women are exclusively fitted. ' In the first place, women have the power of pleasing. Accomplishments are cultivated as instrumental to the successful exercise of this power, and therefore are not to be rejected on the ground that they waste the time that might be given to mathematics. The common sense of the world has long ago settled that men are to be pleased, and women are to please. Accordingly women acquire an agreeable expertness at the piano, and view the acquisition as a solemn duty.' Another, in answer to the question, what ought all young ladies to learn, says, 'Accomplishments are quite a secondary matter. If men do not get tired of the songs, they soon get tired of the singer, if she can do nothing but sing. What is really wanted in a woman is, that she should be a permanently pleasant companion. So far as education can give or enhance pleasantness, it does so by making the view of life wide, the wit ready, the faculty of comprehension vivid.'

One authority, delightfully contented with things as they are, assures us that, 'humanly speaking, the best sort of British young lady is all that a woman can be expected to be—civil, intelligent, enthusiastic, decorous, and, as a rule, prettier than in any other country. We are perfectly satisfied with what we have got.' Another, less happily constituted, asserts that 'all good judges and good teachers lament the present system of girls' education. It is all cramming, and with such very poor results. After all is over, girls know very little and care about less. Most girls are decidedly stupid, and what good can cramming of the most barren and repulsive kind do to stupid girls? We should consider what we want women to be. That they should be trained to be good and generous is by far the first thing. . . . The next thing is that they should be well-mannered and healthy. The third requisite is, that they should know how to express themselves—should have a right standard in judging books and men, and

public and private life. . . . The fourth
requisite is, that they should know how to
bear rule in a household. . . . These are all
the essentials.'

Another view is, that a woman should
be 'a gentle tyrant, capricious indeed, yet
generous and kindhearted withal, varying
in mood, now clouded, now serene, though
given less to tears than laughter, and
bright with gleams of hopeful sunshine
like the spring. She should be no dunce,
no ignoramus, this enviable woman ; she
should not have stopped in her education
when the governess's back was turned, nor
hold that to play Mr Chappell's music
creditably is the one aim and end of all
instruction ; she should know enough to
take her part in topics of general conver-

sation, to read the *Times* with interest, and talk about the leading article without a yawn; she should be fond enough of learning to find that her leisure seldom hangs heavy on her hands; and if (though it is almost too much to expect) she has sufficient patience with the process of induction to be able to reason on any subject for two minutes together without jumping to a conclusion either way, we may well congratulate ourselves on having drawn the great prize in the lottery of life.' Mr Coventry Patmore seems to prefer that the gentle tyranny and the capriciousness should be on the other side.

'He who toils all day,
And comes home hungry, tired or cold,
And feels 'twould do him good to scold

His wife a little, let him trust
Her love, and boldly be unjust,
And not care till she cries!   How prove
In any other way his love
Till soothed in mind by meat and rest?
If, after that, she's well caress'd,
And told how good she is to bear
His humour, fortune makes it fair.
Women like men to be like men,
That is, at least, just now and then!'

The wife is here represented as rejoicing in her husband's ill-temper, as affording her an opportunity of dispelling it by soothing arts, a practical illustration, it may be observed, of the complementary theory, the woman's patience actually demanding a man's sulkiness to practise upon. Contrast Mr Patmore's 'Jane' with Mr Tennyson's 'Isabel.'

'Eyes not down-dropt nor over-bright, but fed
With the clear-pointed flame of chastity,

Clear, without heat, undying, tended by
Pure vestal thoughts in the translucent fane
Of her still spirit; locks not wide-dispread,
Madonna-wise on either side her head;
Sweet lips whereon perpetually did reign
The summer calm of golden charity,
Were fixed shadows of thy fixed mood,
   Revered Isabel, the crown and head,
The stately flower of female fortitude,
   Of perfect wifehood and pure lowlihead.

'The intuitive decision of a bright
  And thorough-edged intellect to part
    Error from crime; a prudence to withhold;
    The laws of marriage character'd in gold
Upon the blanched tablets of her heart;
A love still burning upward, giving light
To read those laws; an accent very low
In blandishment, but a most silver flow
    Of subtle-paced counsel in distress,
Right to the heart and brain, though undescried,
    Winning its way with extreme gentleness
Through all the outworks of suspicious pride;
A courage to endure and to obey;
A hate of gossip parlance, and of sway,
Crown'd Isabel, through all her placid life,
The queen of marriage, a most perfect wife.'

The self-defence which Shakespeare puts
into the mouth of Queen Katherine de-
scribes a different type :—

> 'Heaven witness
> I have been to you a true and humble wife,
> At all times to your will conformable ;
> Ever in fear to kindle your dislike,
> Yea, subject to your countenance ; glad or sorry,
> As I saw it incline. When was the hour
> I ever contradicted your desire,
> Or made it not mine too ? or which of your friends
> Have I not strove to love, although I knew
> He were mine enemy ? what friend of mine
> That had to him derived your anger, did I
> Continue in my liking ? nay, gave notice
> He was from thence discharged ?'

This picture of trembling devotion, of
'distrust qualified by fear,' appears in a
selection called 'Beautiful Poetry,' under
the heading 'A True Wife.' But this
kind of wife would be positively disliked
by some husbands. It has been said that

'perhaps—such is masculine nature—a wife with more knowledge, more fixity of thought, and more general mental power than one's-self might be "a blessing in disguise." But one who is goose enough to sympathise at random on subjects of which she knows little or nothing, because it is "feminine" to do so, is a nuisance *not* in disguise. . . . For our own part, we would just as soon have the sympathy of a chameleon as that of a woman who lives completely in particulars, and is quite destitute of power to appreciate a universal principle.'

These are but a few samples, culled almost at random from the mass of contradictory evidence to be found in English literature. Conceive a governess or school-

mistress, duly impressed with the obligation
of training her pupils to be accomplished
pleasers of men, and trying to fashion for
them a model out of such materials! Must
not the result be simply blank despair?
The same conclusion might be reached by
a shorter process. Men are supposed to
marry the sort of women they like. But
looking upon the infinite variety of wives
to be met with in society, could any one
generalise from them a model wife, who
might serve as a pattern to educators?
Would any man wish for a wife so mo-
delled? Might it not be as well to abandon this distracting theory—to discard the
shifting standard of opinion, and to fall
back upon the old doctrine which teaches
educators to seek in every human soul for

that divine image which it is their work to call out and to develope ?

The educational question depends, as we have seen, on the larger question of women's place in the social order. Are they to be regarded, and to regard themselves, primarily as children of God, members of Christ, and heirs of the kingdom of heaven, and, secondarily, as wives, mothers, daughters, sisters ? or are the family relationships to overshadow the divine and the social, and to be made the basis of a special moral code, applying to women only ? According to the first view, all human duties—everything that is lovely and of good report—all moral virtues and all Christian graces are inculcated and enforced by the highest sanctions. An ascetic contempt for wifely and motherly and daughterly ties is no part of the Christian ideal. But the view which teaches women to think of family claims as embracing their whole duty—which bids them choose to serve man rather than God—sets before them a standard of obligation which, in proportion as it is exclusively adhered to, vitiates not their lives only, but those of the men on whom their influence might be of a far different sort. That such a theory is radically inconsistent with the divine order might easily be shown. That its action on society is profoundly demoralising is a lesson taught by mournful experience.

CHAPTER III.

THINGS AS THEY ARE.

WHETHER it is owing to the prevailing confusion of ideas as to the objects of female education, or to whatever cause it may be attributed, there can be little doubt that the thing itself is held in slight esteem. No one indeed would go so far as to say that it is not worth while to educate girls at all. *Some* education is held to be indispens-

able, but how much is an open question ;
and the general indifference operates in
the way of continually postponing it to
other claims, and, above all, in shortening
the time allotted to systematic instruction
and discipline. Parents are ready to make
sacrifices to secure a tolerably good and
complete education for their sons ; they
do not consider it necessary to do the
same for their daughters. Or perhaps it
would be putting it more fairly to say,
that a very brief and attenuated course of
instruction, beginning late and ending
early, is believed to constitute a good and
complete education for a woman.

It is usually assumed that when a boy's
school education has once begun, which
it does at a very early age, it is to go on

steadily till he is a man. A boy who leaves
school at sixteen or eighteen, either enters
upon some technical course of training for
a business or profession, or he passes on to
the University, and from thence to active
work of some sort or other. In other
words, he is *in statu pupillari* until general education and professional instruction
are superseded by the larger education
supplied by the business of life. In the
education of girls no such regular order
appears. A very usual course seems to
be for girls to spend their early years in a
haphazard kind of way, either at home,
or in not very regular attendance at an
inferior school ; after which they are sent
for a year or two to a school or college to
finish. The heads of schools complain

with one voice that they are called upon
to 'finish' what has never been begun,
and that to attempt to give anything like
a sound education, in the short time at
their disposal, is perfectly hopeless. But,
to take the most favourable case,—that of
a girl so well prepared that she is able to
make good use of the teaching provided in
a first-rate school,—just at the moment
when she is making real, substantial progress, she is taken away. At sixteen,
seventeen, or eighteen, as the case may be,
her education comes to an abrupt pause.
When she marries, it may be said to begin
again ; but between leaving school and
marriage there is usually an interval of at
least three or four years, if not a much
longer period. These years a youth

spends, as has been before said, in preparation for his future career. In the case of girls, no such preparation seems to be considered necessary.

Is this reasonable? Apart from immediate pecuniary necessity, is it desirable that the regular education of women should be considered as finished at the age of eighteen? If we are to take the almost universal practice as an answer, it is a very decided affirmative. Even girls whose parents must be fully aware that they will eventually have to maintain themselves, seldom receive any adequate training for their future work. Those whose fathers intend to provide for them, are still less likely to be supposed to want any further education after they leave school.

So fixed and wide-spread a custom must
have had, at some time or other, even if it
has not now, a meaning and a justification.
And this may perhaps be found in the fact
that our mothers and our grandmothers
were accustomed to undergo at home,
after leaving school, what was in fact an
apprenticeship to household management.
It seems indeed at one time to have been
customary to apprentice girls of what we
now call the middle class, to trades,—as
we find George Herbert urging his Country
Parson not to put his children 'into vain
trades and unbefitting the reverence of
their father's calling, such as are taverns for
men and lacemaking for women,'—but
even where there was no apprenticeship to
a specific business, the round of house-

hold labours would supply a very considerable variety of useful occupation. An active part in these labours would naturally devolve upon the daughters of the house, who would thus be forming habits of industry and order invaluable in after life.

Probably a great many fathers, profoundly ignorant as they are of the lives of women, cherish a vague imagination that the same kind of thing is going on still. If Providence should at any time lead them to spend a week in the society of their daughters, under ordinary circumstances—not when illness has altered the usual current of affairs—they would find that this is very far from being the case. That great male public, which

spends its days in chambers and offices
and shops, knows little of what is going
on at home. Writers in newspapers and
magazines are fond of talking about the
nursery, as if every household contained
a never-ending supply of young children,
on whom the grown-up daughters might
be practising the art of bringing up.
Others have a great deal to say about
the kitchen, assuming it to be desirable
that the ladies of the house should super-
sede, or at least assist, the cook. In that
case, where there is a mother with two or
three daughters, we should have four or
five cooks. The undesirableness of such
a multiplication of artists need scarcely
be pointed out.* Needlework, again,

* As this pursuit is sometimes recommended with

occupies a much larger space in the imagination of writers than it does in practical life. Except in families where there are children, there is very little plain needlework to be done, and what there is, many people make a point of giving out, on the ground that it is better to pay a half-starved needlewoman for work done, than to give her the money in the form of alms.

apparent seriousness, it may be as well to point out to the uninitiated, that if mistresses are to do the cooking, masters must dine alone. Dinners cannot be cooked an hour beforehand, and left to serve themselves up. In this, as in other arts, the finishing touches are among the most important. This does not mean, of course, that a mistress may not give directions and occasional help, or that it may not be a very good thing for girls to lend a hand, now and then, by way of learning to cook. That is a different thing from regularly spending a considerable part of their daily lives in the kitchen.

Having mentioned needlework, cookery, and the care of children, we seem to have come to an end of the household work in which ladies are supposed to take part. If young women of eighteen and upwards are learning anything in their daily life at home, it must be something beside and beyond the acquirement of dexterity in ordinary domestic arts.

Many fathers, however, are no doubt aware that their daughters have very little to do. But that seems to them anything but a hardship. They wish they had a little less to do themselves, and can imagine all sorts of interesting pursuits to which they would betake themselves if only they had a little more leisure. Ladies, it may be said, have their choice, and they must evidently prefer idleness, or they would find something to do. If this means that half-educated young women do not choose steady work when they have no inducement whatever to overcome natural indolence, it is no doubt true. Women are not stronger - minded than men, and a commonplace young woman can no more work steadily without motive or discipline than a commonplace young man. It has been remarked that 'the active, voluntary part of man is very small, and if it were not economised by a sleepy kind of habit, its results would be null. We could not do every day out of our own heads all we have to do. We should accomplish nothing; for all our energies would be frittered away in minor attempts at petty improvement.' The case of young women could scarcely have been better stated. Every day they have to do out of their own heads nearly all that they have to do. They accomplish little; for their energies are frittered away in minor attempts at petty improvement.

How true this is, the friends and counsellors of girls could abundantly testify. There is no point on which schoolmistresses are more unanimous and more emphatic than on the difficulty of knowing what to do with girls after leaving school. People who have not been brought into intimate converse with young women have little idea of the extent to which they suffer from perplexities of conscience. 'The discontent of the modern girl' is not mere

D

idle self-torture. Busy men and women
—and people with disciplined minds—can
only, by a certain strain of the imagination, conceive the situation. If they at all
entered into it, they could not have the
heart to talk as they do. For the case of
the modern girl is peculiarly hard in this,
that she has fallen upon an age in which
idleness is accounted disgraceful. The
social atmosphere rings with exhortations
to act, act in the living present. Everywhere we hear that true happiness is to be
found in work—that there can be no leisure without toil—that people who do
nothing are unfruitful fig-trees which
cumber the ground. And in this atmosphere the modern girl lives and breathes.

She is not a stone, and she does not live underground. She hears people talk—she listens to sermons—she reads books. And in her reading she comes across such passages as the following :—

'It is a real pleasure to me to find that you are taking steadily to a profession, without which I scarcely see how a man can live honestly. That is, I use the term "profession" in rather a large sense, not as simply denoting certain callings which a man follows for his maintenance, but rather a definite field of duty, which the nobleman has as much as the tailor, but which he has not, who having an income large enough to keep him from starving, hangs about upon life, merely following his own caprices and fancies ; *quod factu pessimum est.'**

Or again :—

' N'est-il pas vrai que la fadeur de la vie est à la fois le grand malheur et le grand danger ? Il y a une douzaine d'années, un orateur s'écriait à la tribune : "La France s'ennuie." Et moi je dis : L'humanité s'ennuie, et son ennui ne date ni d'aujourd'hui ni d'hier, quoique peut-être il n'ait jamais été plus visible qu'en ce moment. Sans la poursuite d'un but idéal, toute vie devient inevitablement insipide, même jusqu'au dégout. Or, comptez parmi vos connaissances les personnes qui poursuivent un but élevé. Beaucoup

---

* Letter to Dr Greenhill, an old pupil, in ' Life of Dr Arnold,' p. 392.

vivent sans savoir pourquoi, uniquement, je pense, parce que chaque matin ramène le soleil. Que de femmes, si vous exceptez les mères qui se donnent à leur famille, que de femmes, hélas, dont la vie se passe entière dans de futiles occupations, ou dans des conversations plus futiles encore ! Et l'on s'étonne que, rongées d'ennui, elles recherchent avec frénésie toutes les distractions imaginables ! Elles accusent la monotonie de leur existence d'être la cause de ce vague malaise ; la vraie cause est ailleurs, elle est dans la fadeur intolérable, non d'une vie dépourvue d'événements et d'aventures, mais d'une vie dont on n'entrevoit pas la raison ni le but. On se sent vivre sans qu'on y soit pour quelque chose, et cette vie inconsciente, inutile, absurde, inspire un mécontentement trop fondé.'*

Such things the modern girl reads, and every word is confirmed by her own experience. With the practical English mind, which she has inherited from her father, she applies it all to herself. She seeks for counsel, and she finds it. She is bidden to 'look around her' — to do the duty that lies nearest—to teach in the schools, or visit the poor—to take up a pursuit—to lay down a course of study and stick to it. She looks around her, and sees no particular call to active exertion. The duties that lie in the way are swallowed up by an energetic mother or elder sister; very possibly she has no

* Sermons par T. Colani.—*Deuxième Recueil*, p. 293.

vocation for philanthropy—and the most devoted philanthropists are the most urgent in warning off people who lack the vocation—or she lives in a village where the children are better taught than she could teach them, and the poor are already too much visited by the clergyman's family ; she feels no sort of impulse to take up any particular pursuit, or to follow out a course of study ; and so long as she is quiet and amiable, and does not get out of health, nobody wants her to do anything.   Her relations and friends— her world—are quite satisfied that she should 'hang about upon life, merely following her own'—or their own—'caprices and fancies.'   The advice given, so easy to offer, so hard to follow, presupposes exactly what is wanting, a formed and disciplined character, able to stand alone, and to follow steadily a predetermined course, without fear of punishment, or hope of reward. Ought we to wonder if, in the great majority of cases, girls let themselves go drifting down the stream, despising themselves, but listlessly yielding to what seems to be their fate ?

An appeal to natural guides is most often either summarily dismissed, or received with reproachful astonishment. It is considered a just cause for surprise and disappointment, that well brought up girls, surrounded with all the comforts of home, should have a wish or a thought extending beyond its precincts. And, perhaps, it is only natural that parents should be slow to encourage their daughters in aspirations after any duties and interests besides those of ministering to their comfort and pleasure. In taking for granted that this is the only object, other than that of marriage, for which women were created, they are but adopting the received sentiment of society. No doubt, too, they honestly believe that, in keeping their daughters to themselves till they marry, they are doing the best thing for them, as well as pleasing themselves. If the daughters take a different view, parents think it is because they are young and inexperienced, and incompetent to judge. The fact is, it is the parents who are inexperienced. Their youth was

different in a hundred ways from the
youth of this generation; and the experience of thirty years ago is far from
being infallible in dealing with the difficulties and perplexities of the present.
No doubt young people are ignorant,
and want guidance. But they should be
helped and advised, not silenced. Parents
take upon themselves a heavy responsi-
bility when they hastily crush the longing
after a larger and more purposeful life.

That such an impulse is worthy of
respect can scarcely be denied. The
existence of capacities is in itself an in-
dication that they are intended for some
good purpose. Conscious power is not a
burden, to be borne with patience, but a
gift, for the due use of which the pos-

sessor rightly feels accountable. To have a soul which can be satisfied with vanities is not eminently virtuous and Christian, but the reverse. To be awake to responsibilities, sensitive in conscience, quickly responsive to all kindling influences, is a sign that education has, so far, done a good work. A flowing river is no doubt more troublesome to manage than a tranquil pool; but pools, if let alone too long, are apt to become noxious, as well as useless. The current may require to be wisely directed; but that there should be a current of being, wanting to set itself somewhere, is surely a cause for thankful rejoicing. It is an unfortunate misunderstanding of the true state of the case that makes parents sigh

over what might well be their happiness
and pride : one more exemplification of
the sluggishness which hates nothing so
bitterly as to be called upon to think—to
consider a new idea—perhaps to go farther,
and take a step out of the beaten track.
It is much easier, no doubt, to say to a
daughter who comes to you with her
original notions—'My dear child, put it
out of your head directly; it cannot be
thought of for a moment'—than it would
be to hear her patiently, to consider how
far her crude ideas are practicable, to
help her, so far as may be, in carrying
them out. And one ought not to wonder
that the easiest course is the one most
commonly chosen. How far it may, or
may not, be the duty of daughters to

sacrifice their own wishes to the temporary pleasure of those to whom they owe so much, is a separate question. It is at least well for parents to know that, far more than they are at all aware of, it is felt to be a sacrifice, and that they must accept it as such, if at all.*

* 'M. de Parthenau would have been surprised had any one suggested that this peaceful life was less to the taste of his children than himself. Like so many excellent fathers, he sincerely believed that because it suited him, it must suit them. He had forgotten his own stormy youth, to find himself happy by his fireside, and it never occurred to him to ask, "Is my daughter happy?" So much the better, since he could have done nothing; and Thérèse was the last person to make him suspect that she was not perfectly satisfied. Yet, whoever had seen her, would have thought her destined for a wider sphere than that of the narrow world where she strove to be content. It had not always been so. Now, however, she stifled all the aspirations, the radiant visions which once haunted her, under the crowd of occupations which she found

The representation here given is, of
course, not universally applicable. It
is quite possible that in some senses, and
to some persons, an apparently empty
life may be easier, and even richer, than
one of toil. There are people to whom
the Happy Valley kind. of life is by no

for herself. She silenced the cry of her intellect, and
yet heard it always ; perhaps because she shunned as
snares the natural outlets which presented themselves,
refusing each rare opportunity of leaving home, lest
she should return discontented ; and putting away
books and pencils, that she might have no interests
but those of her father and her poor dependents. It
was an honest, mistaken effort to do right; and the
confessor, who stood to her in the place of a conscience, approved it—nay, urged it on her. It was
strange, this mute, ceasless conflict, known only in
its full extent to herself, and hidden under so monotonous and peaceful a life !'—*Sydonie's Dowry*, p. 24.

May not something like a counterpart of this mute,
ceasless conflict be hidden under many a monotonous
and peaceful English life ?

means intolerable; and even earnest-
minded and conscientious girls, urged by
a strong sense of the heinousness of discontent, often manage to crush troublesome aspirations, and make themselves
happy. There is something undignified
in being miserable, without a just and
intelligible cause to show for it; and
many young women, capable of higher
things, accommodate themselves with a
considerable degree of cheerfulness to a
narrow and unsatisfying round of existence. Nor is it intended to represent
ladies as habitually doing nothing. On
the contrary, they have many resources.
Among them are various arts and handi-
crafts, gardening, letter-writing, and much
reading. Of these, the last is perhaps the

most popular and the most delusive. A
girl who is 'very fond of reading' is
considered to be happily suited with
never-failing occupation, and no thought
is taken as to what is to come of her
reading. On this subject, the observations of Miss Aikin, herself an experienced
reader, are worth considering. 'Continual reading,' she says, 'if desultory,
and without a definite object, favours indolence, unsettles opinions, and of course
enfeebles the mental and moral energies.'
And Mr Robertson of Brighton, speaking
in reference to girls, remarks that they
'read too much, and think too little. I
will answer for it that there are few girls
of eighteen who have not read more books
than I have. . . . That multifarious read-

ing weakens the mind more than doing
nothing; for it becomes a necessity at
last, like smoking, and is an excuse for
the mind to lie dormant, whilst thought
is poured in, and runs through, a clear
stream, over unproductive gravel, on
which not even mosses grow. It is
the idlest of all idlenesses, and leaves
more of impotency than any other.' •

The same might be said of all merely
dilettante occupation. Its fault is simply
that it *is dilettante*—literally a pastime.
It may as well be done, if nothing else
turns up, and that is all. And this drawback, belonging to nearly all the ordinary
work of young women, they are by themselves unable to overcome. Of course,
the case is partly in their own hands,

E

and those who are by nature abnormally energetic, will make a career for themselves in spite of difficulties. Where the inward impulse is irrepressible, it becomes a lantern to the feet, and a lamp unto the path, making the way of duty plain and unmistakable. But for the few whose course is thus illumined, there will be the many hovering in uneasy doubt, their consciences and intellects just lively enough to make them restless and unhappy, not sufficiently clear in their minds as to right and wrong, either to be nerved for vigorous action, or to accept contentedly the conventional duty of quiescence. There must be something wrong in social regulations which make a demand for exceptional wisdom and strength on the part of any particular class; and that such a demand is made upon average young women is sufficiently clear. What society says to them seems to be something to this effect. Either you have force enough to win a place in the world, in the face of heavy discouragement, or you have not. If you have, the discipline of the struggle is good for you; if you have not, you are not worth troubling about. Is not this a hard thing to say to commonplace girls, not professing to be better or stronger than their neighbours? Why should their task be made, by social and domestic arrangements, peculiarly and needlessly difficult? And why should it be taken for granted that, if they fail, they

must. be extraordinarily silly or self-in-
dulgent? More than any other class,
at the same age, they are exempted
from direction and control — liberally
gifted with the kind of freedom enjoyed
by the denizens of a village pound.
Within their prescribed sphere, they may
wander at will, and if they 'there small
scope for action see,' it is explained to
them that they must not 'for this give
room to discontent;'. nor let their time
'be spent in idly dreaming' how they
might be

> 'More free
> From outward hindrance or impediment.
> For presently this hindrance thou shalt find
> That without which all goodness were a task
> So slight, that virtue never could grow strong.'

In reply to such admonitions they are

tempted to inquire what task, other than
that of dreaming, is set before them—
what virtue, always excepting that one
virtue of passive submission, has any
chance of growing strong under such
conditions. The 'slow,' who sink into
dull inertia, and the 'fast,' who get rid
of their superfluous energy in silly ex-
travagances, have alike the excuse, that
at the moment when they need the support of a routine explained and justified
by a reasonable purpose, discipline and
stimulus are at once withdrawn, leaving
in their place no external support beyond
the trivial demands and restraints of conventional society.

It may seem that an exaggerated importance is here attached to the interval

between school and marriage ; and if the considerations brought forward had reference to this period only, the charge would be just. But rightly to estimate the value of these years, we must bear in mind that they are the spring-time of life —the season of blossom, on which the fruit of the future depends. It is then that an impress is given to character which lasts through life. Opportunities then thrown away or misused can scarcely be recovered in later years. And it has seemed necessary to dwell upon the existing tenour of young women's lives, because, in dealing with the question of extending the duration of female education, we must be largely influenced by our conception of the alternative involved

in leaving things as they are. It has
been said that the end of education is
'to form a nation of living, orderly men.'
If it has been shown that the course now
pursued tends to make a large part of the
nation inanimate and disorderly, a case
would seem to be established for urging
efforts at improvement.

CHAPTER IV.

THINGS AS THEY MIGHT BE.

SUPPOSING so much to be granted, it will be asked, What can be done? Clearly, girls cannot be kept at school indefinitely till they marry. When they leave school, say at eighteen, what are they to do next? The answer must chiefly depend on circumstances. Where the resources of the parents are such that there is a reasonable

certainty of an abundant provision for the
future, an education corresponding with
that given by the universities to young
men—in other words, ' the education of a
lady,' considered irrespectively of any
specific uses to which it may afterwards
be turned—would appear to be the desi-
deratum.   And clearly ' the education of
a lady' ought to mean the highest and the
finest culture of the time.   The accurate
habits of thought and the intellectual po-
lish by which the scholar is distinguished,
ought to be no less carefully sought in
the training of women than in that of
men.   This would be true, even if only for
the sake of the charm which high culture
gives to social intercourse, a charm attainable in no other way.   But apart from

this consideration, the duties of women of
the higher class are such as to demand
varied knowledge as well as a disciplined
mind and character. Difficult cases in
social ethics frequently arise, on which
women are obliged to act and to guide the
action of others. However incompetent
they may be, they cannot escape the re-
sponsibility of judging and deciding. And
though natural sagacity and the happy
impulses of which we hear so much often
come to their aid, prejudice and mistaken
impulses ought also to be taken into the
account as disturbing elements of a very
misleading kind. In dealing with social
difficulties, the value of a cultivated judgment, able to unravel entangled evidence,
and to give due weight to a great variety

of conflicting considerations, would seem to be obvious enough. It would be well worth while to exchange the wonderful unconscious instinct, by which women are supposed to leap to right conclusions, no one knows how, for the conscious power of looking steadily and comprehensively at the whole facts of a case, and thereupon shaping a course of action, with a clear conception of its probable issues. Of course, a merely literary education will not give this power. Knowledge of the world and of human nature, only to be gained by observation and experience, go farther than mere knowledge of books. But the habit of impartiality and deliber- ation—of surveying a wide field of thought —and of penetrating, so far as human eye can see, into the heart of things—which is promoted by genuine study even of books alone—tends to produce an attitude of mind favourable for the consideration of complicated questions of any sort. A comparison between the judgment of a scholar and that of an uneducated man on matters requiring delicate discrimination and grasp of thought, shows the degree in which the intellect may be fitted by training for tasks of this nature. A large and liberal culture is probably also the best corrective of the tendency to take petty views of things, and on this account is especially to be desired for women on whom it devolves to give the tone to ' society.'

How far it may be desirable or justifiable for women to take part in political affairs is a vexed question, into which it is the less necessary here to enter, inasmuch as it is evident that the same kind of intellectual training which forms the groundwork of the education of a statesman is needed for other purposes. Women who think at all can scarcely help thinking about the condition of the poor, and to arrive at sound conclusions on so vast a subject involves an acquaintance more or less complete with almost every consideration which comes within the range of the politician. Unpaid work, such as the management of hospitals, workhouses, prisons and reformatories, and charitable societies, naturally devolves upon the leisurely classes, and which has been brought before Parliament during the last few years, on which it is not as directly important that right opinions should be formed by women as by men.

The higher education already spoken of would serve as a preparation for literary work, and as a groundwork for more definite technical instruction in every department of art. And, lastly, an extended course of study is, above all things, necessary for those who are to undertake the office of teaching others. The incompleteness of the education of schoolmistresses and governesses is a drawback which no amount of intelligence and goodwill can enable them entirely to overcome. It is obvious that for those who have to impart knowledge the primary requisite is to possess it; and it is one of the great difficulties of female teachers that they are called upon to instruct others, while very inadequately instructed themselves. The more earnest and conscientious devote their leisure hours to continued study, and, no doubt, much may be done in this way; but it is at the cost of overwork, often involving the sacrifice of health, to say nothing of the disadvantages of working alone, without a teacher, often without good books, and without the wholesome stimulus of companionship.

These considerations lead up to the more distinctly professional side of the question, that which relates to the pur-

F

suit of any particular calling as a means of maintenance. Every one knows that there are women, some even of the upper class, who must earn their own living; and this being admitted, it will scarcely be disputed that they ought to be put into the best way of doing it. The thing to find out seems to be what professions are there, taking the word as including business of all sorts, to which they might betake themselves with a fair prospect of success? Perhaps we may gain some light by looking into history, and seeing what went on in earlier times, before the advance of science, with its infinite subdivisions of labour, had made it almost impossible to carry on any profitable pursuit within the precincts of home.

Confining ourselves, for the sake of brevity, to English history, we find among the ordinary avocations of women Medicine and Surgery, including the compounding and dispensing of drugs ; the service of the afflicted and distressed in mind, body, or estate ; farming ; marketing ; and a variety of domestic manufactures, too numerous to recite in detail.

Would the same pursuits, under regulations adapted to altered conditions, be proper for women now ? Among those which have been mentioned, that of Medicine appears peculiarly desirable, as affording scope for the exercise of the highest gifts, in a field in which women's close acquaintance with the details of domestic life would be a valuable adjunct.

The medical profession is now accessible to any competent woman who is able to defray the cost of instruction. The licence of the Court of Apothecaries, which constitutes a legal qualification for general practice, is given on passing the required examinations. There is no difficulty in the way of apprenticeship, and lectures and hospital practice are attainable, though at a higher cost to individual students, than would be incurred if the expense were divided among several. The objection often urged against the practice of medicine by women, that they have no confidence in each other, and that a medical woman would therefore find herself without patients, can only be conclusively answered by facts. *À priori*, there is some reason to believe, that, always assuming the education to be equally thorough and equally well attested, the services of a lady will be preferred; but till women have full opportunity of choice, it is impossible to say positively what they will choose. The experience of a few years will decide. In the meantime, Miss Garrett's very remarkable success is at least encouraging to other aspirants in the same field.

Closely allied to the practice of medicine are the functions of educated women in ministering to the poor, the insane, and the criminal. These services, so far as they are paid, are now chiefly carried on in workhouses, hospitals, reformatories, and penitentiaries. The superintendence of nurses and the offices of matron and schoolmistress are in the hands of women, and there seems room for further development in this direction. It may be a question for consideration whether in some cases it might not be desirable to substitute the services of an educated Christian lady for those of the chaplain. The duties of a workhouse chaplain are thus defined by the Poor-Law Board :—

'ART. 211. *Duties of the Chaplain.*

'The following shall be the duties of the chaplain :—

'No. 1. To read prayers, and preach a sermon to the paupers and other inmates of the workhouse on every Sunday, and on Good Friday and Christmas-day, unless the guardians, with the consent of the commissioners, may otherwise direct.

'No. 2. To examine the children, and to catechise such as belong to the Church of England, at least once in every month, and to make a record of the same, and state the dates of his attendance, the general progress and condition of the children, and the moral and religious state of the inmates generally, in a book to be kept for that purpose, to be laid before the guardians at their next ordinary meeting, and to be termed "The Chaplain's Report."

'No. 3. To visit the sick paupers, and to administer religious consolation to them in the workhouse, at such periods as the guardians may appoint, and when applied to for that purpose by the master or matron.'

The work laid out under the two last clauses might certainly be done as well, in some respects perhaps better, by a duly qualified lady; and on the face of it, there seems to be no particular reason why paupers should not attend their parish church and be visited by the clergyman like other parishioners. The desirableness of workhouse visiting by ladies has been much discussed, and is now beginning to be acknowledged. The presence of a lady in an official capacity might be still more valuable, both as being permanent and as waiving the difficulties which are so apt to come in the way of philanthropic interference in state institutions. A lady appointed expressly by the guardians themselves could scarcely provoke jealousy, and her representations, based on thorough knowledge of the matter in hand, and modified by sympathy with the difficulties and scruples of authorities, as well as with the claims of the suffering, would be comparatively exempt from the charge of officiousness. That she would naturally gather round her such helpers as she might need in an unofficial capacity is an obvious advantage. The same observations would seem to be applicable to hospitals and prisons, and all public institutions where women are employed in a subordinate capacity. That the presence and the active influence of a lady, by whatever name she might be called, would be a valuable element, wherever the sick in mind or body are congregated together, is

generally admitted, though the theory has not in England been acted upon to any considerable extent.

Next in our enumeration comes the business of farming. The social prejudice against useful occupations of any sort, as distinguished from those which are supposed to be ornamental, has here been actively at work. The superintendence of farming operations is still, however, largely shared by women, especially in the north of England. In commercial dealings there is a good deal of work to be done which could not, at any rate in our present very imperfect state of civilisation, be properly undertaken by women. There are, however, branches of mercantile and quasi-mercantile business, including that profession of modern growth which has been called 'management,'—in which wise arrangements, carefully made, are all that is required to make them suitable. In almost every kind of business, wholesale and retail, the book-keeping and the correspondence might be very fitly carried on by competent women.

With regard to the manufactures which now form so vast a portion of our national industry, a great revolution has taken place, and it is here, above all, that a re-adjustment of social and domestic arrangements, involving some innovation on conventional ideas and usages, seems to be imperatively needed. Down to a comparatively recent period, every household was a workshop. It is within the present generation that the sewing-machine has laid hold of the last remaining implement of domestic manufacture. The home is no longer a manufactory. Spinning, weaving, knitting, sewing, all are gone, or going. What has become of the busy hands and brains? The hands are gone into factories, the brains are idle. We cannot call back the hands, and again set them to work in the domestic manufactory. Might it not be possible to bring them again under womanly influence, and at the same time find fit work for the brains, by introducing women of the employing class into factories? Might we not restore the old order of things, under which the payers of wages and the receivers of wages worked together, to the

mutual advantage of both—by replacing
women in the position of directors and
overlookers of female labour ?   It is vain
to say that a factory is not a fit place for
a lady.   If it is not, it ought to be made
so.   If the moral atmosphere of a workshop is necessarily debasing, no human
being ought to be exposed to its influence.
But is it *necessarily* debasing ?   Are ma-
chines in themselves demoralising ?   What
is the moral difference between a spin-
ning-jenny and a distaff ?   Are knitting-
needles refined, and knitting-machines
coarse ?   Is there any reason, in the
nature of things, why the moral tone of
a factory should be less pure and elevating than that of the home ?   Is it not
rather that we want, in our modern

workshops, the influence conveyed by
daily intercourse between women to
whom wealth has given the means of
culture and refinement, and the labourers
whom poverty obliges to work with their
hands, but who need not therefore part
with any essential feminine attribute?
If, in all the works where women are
employed in the inferior departments, the
daughters of the masters were instructed
in the business, made so thoroughly con-
versant with it as to be able to take a
real part in its direction, two advantages
would be gained.   The higher class of
workers would acquire larger sympathies,
more living interests, increased aptitude
for affairs, and an exhilarating sense of
usefulness — of having a place in the

world from which they would be missed
if they were withdrawn from it. The
lower class would, on their part, be
elevated by the contact with a genuine
refinement, not too 'fine' to be useful.
They would see that a lady is a lady, not
in virtue of her costly dress and luxurious
habits, but in the gentleness, the truth-
fulness, and the sensitive sympathy, which
are among the most precious fruits of
high culture. And it can scarcely be
doubted that such an example, such an
ideal, brought within the immediate and
daily contemplation of women and girls
of the labouring class, would be more
effectual in rectifying their standard of
morals and refinement than any philanthropic agency, however well-intentioned

and judicious, which could be brought to bear from without. In some cases there might be difficulties in the way of teaching women the practical parts of a manufacture, but there can be few businesses in which some place might not be found for them. Even where female labourers are not employed in the lower departments — though there the case is the strongest—women might often take part in the direction, with great advantage to themselves, and at least without injury to any one else.

It appears, then, that a transference of the scene of action, and an accommodation of old principles and practices to new circumstances, is the task of the present generation, and the true answer to the appeal of women for something to do. The change proposed, so far from being a departure from the old ways, is, in fact, a recurrence to them. The advocates of things as they are, are the innovators. Those who sigh after things as they might be, are the old-fashioned people, eager to retain, with only such modifications as advancing civilisation has made indispensable, all that is best in things as they were.

G

CHAPTER V.

PROFESSIONAL AND DOMESTIC LIFE.

AN obvious rejoinder to the foregoing suggestions will at once present itself. It will be said that professions and business may be all very well—may indeed be best—for single women, but that sooner or later the great majority marry, and any plan of life which fails to recognise this contingency is unpractical and absurd. This is most true. We have to deal with facts; and it is a most important, though not the sole question, How would a higher education and professional training act upon family life? Home duties fall to the lot of almost every woman, and nothing which tends to incapacitate for the performance of them ought to be encouraged. Let us ask, then, what are the home duties of women as such, and what are the qualifications required for their discharge? And here we must remember that the claims involved in the conjugal and parental and filial relations are not special to women. They are not, indeed, to be disregarded in considering the bearing of a scheme of education; but in the discussion of the home duties of women *as such*, it is convenient to treat separately those which are not shared by men.

If we bring before our mind's eye the picture of an English home, we see that the household work is divided between the mistress and the servants. Where there are grown-up daughters, they sometimes help the mistress in her work, or the servants in theirs, but they have no distinct functions of their own. It appears, then, that in an inquiry relating to the upper and middle classes, the only home duties special to women which can come under review, are those of the mistress of the household. What are her functions? Those of government and administration. All housekeepers will agree that this is the work they have to do, though they may not be accustomed to call it by these names. The inexperienced mistress complains, not that she does not know how to cook, or to sew, or to keep the furniture in order—these arts, if she wants them, can be quickly acquired; her perplexity is how to manage the servants. To draw the line between necessary subordination and vexatious interference—to apportion to each a fair share of work, and to see that the work is done—to be liberal and considerate without over-indulgence,—these are duties requiring judgment, moderation, method, decision, often no small share of moral courage; in other words, precisely the same qualities which are wanted in governing bodies of workpeople. In

administration also, it is obvious that,
though on a different scale, the same
sagacity, prudence, and foresight which
would make a woman successful in business, would conduce to the economical
management of domestic concerns.

The head of a household wants an ideal
to work up to, and the governing and
administrative power which will enable
her to carry out her idea.   Here, as else-
where, motive is the primary requisite.
A woman to whom huggermugger is intolerable will find means of escaping from
it—if necessary, by the labour of her own
hands—more often, perhaps, by the skilful
direction of the labour of others.   But
one who has no inner sense of the beauty
of order, to whom the rhythmic flow of a

well-governed household is an unmeaning
conception, or who lacks the gift of mas-
tery over details, may be cooking and
sewing and looking after things from
morning till night ; she may be anxiously
obedient to conventional regulations, rigid
in the observance of ceremonies unmeaning in themselves or unsuited to her position ; with all her striving, she will never
realise the vision of an ideal English
home.

It appears, then, that first, imagination, combined with a certain sensitiveness
of refinement, and secondly, the faculty
of government and administration, are
the qualifications chiefly necessary for
the performance of home duties. No
education can be relied upon as infallibly

securing these rare gifts ; but it may be
assumed that extensive reading of the
best books tends to cultivate imagination
and refinement, and that a life of active
exertion tends to bring out the qualities
which go to make up the governing and
administrative faculty; and if so, a liberal
education and the pursuit of a profession
are perhaps, on the whole, the best training that the conditions of modern society
can supply for the special functions of
the mistress of a household.

It will, however, be pointed out by
practical people, that even supposing the
training to be good as regards domestic
life, parents will not throw away their
money on a costly preparation for a profession which is most likely to be aban-

doned in a few years ; and again, that the
contingency of marriage is likely to act as
a discouragement to girls, making them
so languid in endeavour, that they would
have small chance of success in a professional career.

To the last objection experience would
not lead us to attach much weight. But
supposing that, either through want of
energy or perseverance, or from any other
deficiency, women should take a low place
in the professional ranks, what then ?
The object of their education would have
been, not to set them on a pinnacle of
distinction, but to make them useful
labourers ; and if this end were attained,
society, at any rate, would have no reason
to complain.

It is true, however, that fathers are likely to hesitate in spending money on what may seem a doubtful speculation as regards pecuniary returns. And if marriage necessarily involves the complete abandonment of a profession, the chances are somewhat against professional education as an investment of capital, though perhaps less so than would at first sight appear. Of course much depends on the amount of money which it is necessary to expend. To take the medical profession, as being, among those which women are likely to enter, the one in which the cost of training is probably the highest—it is a liberal computation to allow £500 as covering the cost of instruction over and above the personal expenses, which would

be going on all the same whether a girl
were being educated or not. Such a sum
would, in three or four years of successful
practice, be recovered, and any further
earnings would be clear gain. No doubt,
in cases of very early marriage, a part or
even the whole of the sum expended would
be sunk; and the result of giving women
professions would probably be, on the
whole, to encourage comparatively early
marriage, partly by bringing persons of
congenial tastes into mutual intercourse,
and partly by rendering marriages possible
which would otherwise be flagrantly im-
prudent. But supposing that a woman
married a rich man before she had begun
to practise, the loss of the sum mentioned
could easily be spared. If she married a

poor man, or a man dependent on an
uncertain income, the sacrifice might be
regarded in the light of a sum paid for
insurance—the provision of a resource in
case of widowhood or other misfortune,
which it is well to have in reserve, though
it may be still better never to want it.

In the meantime, however, does marriage necessarily involve giving up a profession ? On the face of it, judging by
existing facts, one would incline to the
contrary view. Some of the highest
names in literature and art are those of
married women ; many schoolmistresses
are married ; clergymen's wives noto-
riously undertake a large share of extra-
domestic work ; and there is no evidence
that in any of these cases the husbands

are neglected, or the children worse brought up than other people's. It seems to be forgotten that women have always been married. Marriage is not a modern discovery, offering a hitherto untrodden field of action for feminine energy. The novelty is, that, as has been said already, the old field has been invaded and taken possession of by machinery. The married ladies of former days, instead of sitting in drawing-rooms, eating the bread of idleness, got through a vast amount of household business, which their successors cannot possibly do, simply because it is not there to be done. An educated woman, of active, methodical habits, blessed with good servants, as good mistresses generally are, finds an hour a day amply sufficient for her housekeeping. Nothing is gained by spreading it out over a longer time.* Allowing a fair margin for what are technically called 'social' claims, there remains a surplus, of course varying very considerably in extent, according to circumstances. The question then arises, whether a married woman, having time and energy to spare, may or may not legitimately spend it, if she likes, either in definitely professional work, or in the unpaid public services, which, when seriously undertaken, constitute something nearly equivalent to a

* On the occasion of a recent vacancy in the secretaryship of a benevolent society several of the candidates were married women. One gave, as her reasons for applying, 'loueliness and want of employment.' In another case, the application was made by a husband on behalf of his wife.

profession. Inasmuch as the adoption of such a course would most probably effect some change in the aspect of family life, it is reasonable to ask whether such change is likely to be for good or for evil; and any objections which may suggest themselves ought to be respectfully considered.

One of the most obvious is the fear that a profession might prove a snare, leading to the neglect of humbler and more irksome duties. And it is right to admit frankly that the apprehension may not be altogether groundless. M. Simon, indeed, asserts, with the happy confidence we are all so apt to display on matters of which we have had no experience, that household drudgery, 'though very laborious, is agreeable to women;' and

Sydney Smith has made merry over the notion that a mother would desert an infant for a quadratic equation. And of course, put in that extreme way, the idea is ridiculous. But looking at the case broadly—putting on one side the little fretting cares and worries of domestic life, and on the other the larger and more genial interests of professional work, it may be confessed that a temptation might very possibly arise to shirk the less engaging task. But it does not follow that because a temptation exists, it must be irresistible. To construct a plan of life absolutely free from temptation is a simple impossibility, even supposing it to be desirable. Every career has its snares, and a life of narrow interests and responsibilities is no exception to the rule. The true safeguard seems to consist, not in restraints and limitations, but in a vivid sense of all that is involved in the closer relationships, and in a steadfast habit of submission to duty. In the present case it may be noted that, however fascinating the temptation may be, it is at any rate open and well understood. It is not a pitfall, which any one could walk into unawares through ignorance of its existence. The paramount importance of home duties is enforced by all the sanctions of an overwhelming public opinion. Any neglect is liable to be punished, not only by the immediate discomfort arising from it, but by universal disapproval. An offence against which the warnings are so

trumpet-tongued, and of which the con-
sequences are so thoroughly disagreeable,
can scarcely be very dangerously attrac-
tive.

If it is admitted that professional
women are likely, or at least as likely as
others, to be both able and diligent in the
discharge of family obligations, another
objection may be raised, founded on the
apprehension that a similarity of pursuits
would produce an unpleasant similarity
between men and women. One of the
most plausible arguments in behalf of dis-
similar education is that which rests on
the general desirableness of variety. We
do not want to be all alike. The course
of civilisation tends, it is said, already too
strongly towards uniformity.

'For "ground in yonder social mill,
We rub each other's angles down,
And lose," he said, "in form and gloss
The picturesque of man and man."'

And if it could be shown that the isolation of the sexes produces variety of the best kind, and to the greatest possible extent, it would no doubt be a strong argument in its favour. But it is questionable whether this is the best means of obtaining variety. As there can be no unanimity on matters of which one party is ignorant, so also, in the same sense, there can be no diversity. We do not obtain two views of a subject by incapacitating one of the parties from taking any view at all. If the differences between men and women are such that they are predisposed to treat whatever comes be-.

fore them in a somewhat different manner, we shall get greater variety by presenting to both the most important subjects of thought, than by sorting out subjects into classes and submitting each to a kind of class treatment. And so also as to methods of training. It seems likely that a more healthily diversified type of character will be obtained by cultivating the common human element, and leaving individual differences free to develop themselves, than by dividing mankind into two great sections and forcing each into a mould. You may indeed obtain diversity by mutilation or distortion. You may make a girl unlike a boy by shutting her up, giving her insufficient air and exercise, and teaching her that grace and refinement are synonymous with affectation and feebleness. You may make a boy unlike a girl by teaching him to care for nothing but out-of-door sports, and by making him believe that he is showing spirit when he is rude and selfish. But this is not the kind of variety that any one seriously wishes to cultivate.

It may here perhaps be argued on the other hand, that to give wives professions would tend to separate them from their husbands by throwing them into a society of their own, and leading them to set up a distinct set of independent interests,— that whereas a wife now throws herself into her husband's concerns, losing sight of herself in her sympathy with him, she would, if she had a pursuit of her own, be led astray by ambition, occupied with her own aims, absorbed in a current of life apart from his. Here again it may be admitted that the danger might, in very rare cases, possibly exist. But, on the whole, the risk seems to be much more than counterbalanced by a very strong tendency in an exactly opposite direction. In many cases, the profession of both would be the same, judging by present experience. Artists marry artists, clergymen's daughters marry clergymen, literary women often, though not always, marry literary men, medical women would probably marry medical men, and so on. It is likely that a man who chose to marry a professional woman at all would marry in his own profession. But supposing it were otherwise, a woman who had work similar, though not in all respects identical with that of her husband, would be more able than one whose occupation was of an entirely alien character, to sympathise with him in his difficulties and in his successes. She would understand them and enter into them with a first-hand kind of interest, fuller and more intelligent, if not more genuine, than a merely reflected interest could be. On the other hand, it would be at least as easy for a husband to enter into interests somewhat akin to his own, as into the small domestic worries which fill so large a space in the thoughts and imaginations of women who have nothing else to occupy them. There are many wives who really have very little to talk to their husbands about, except the virtues or the crimes of servants, and the little gossip of the neighbourhood. If their husbands will not listen to what they have to say on these subjects, they are obliged to take refuge in silence.

The enormous loss to general culture entailed by the solitude of the male intellect is very little thought of. Yet it would seem obvious enough that children brought up in a home where the everyday conversation is of a somewhat thoughtful and literary cast, have an immense start as compared with those who learn nothing unconsciously, and are obliged to gather all their knowledge laboriously from books. Social and domestic intercourse is an educational instrument largely used in

cultivated circles. In the great mass of
English society it is scarcely used at all,
for this obvious reason, that education is
in great part onesided, and the easy inter-
change of thought is therefore impossible.
A slight infusion of an intellectual element
would go far to expel the gossip and the
microscopic criticism of one's neighbours,
which forms so large and so degrading a
part in the domestic talk of the middle
classes. The mental effort need not be a
severe one. Talk may be very small, and
yet have a certain dignity, if it touches
even but lightly on elevating subjects. It
is the effort to draw up conversation from
empty wells that wearies the spirit, and
drives even goodnatured people into
scandal and slander. Contrast the forced

and insipid small talk of ordinary society, resorted to by way of recreation, but in the last degree unrefreshing in its nature, with the spontaneous overflowings of a cultivated mind.

> 'She spake such good thoughts natural, as if she
>   always thought them—
> She had sympathies so rapid, open, free as bird on
>   branch,
> Just as ready to fly east as west, whichever way be-
>   sought them,
> In the birchen wood a chirrup, or a cock-crow in the
>   grange.
> In her utmost lightness there is truth—and often she
>   speaks lightly,
> Has a grace in being gay, which even mournful souls
>   approve ;
> For the root of some grave earnest thought is under-
>   struck so rightly,
> As to justify the foliage and the waving flowers above.'

It is in fact as a means of bringing men and women together, and bridging over the intellectual gulf between them, that a more liberal education and a larger scope for women are chiefly to be desired. It has been pointed out by a well-known essayist, that ' the purpose of education is not always to foster natural gifts, but sometimes to bring out faculties that might otherwise remain dormant ; and especially so far as to make the persons educated cognisant of excellence in those faculties in others.' And even supposing it could be proved that the separate systems are eminently successful in developing certain peculiarly masculine or feminine gifts, the result would be dearly purchased by the sacrifice of mutual understanding and appreciation.

Oddly enough, it is often assumed that

the only way of getting husbands and wives to agree is to keep them well apart. Common ground, it is taken for granted, must of course be a battle ground. If the theory of the peculiarly receptive character of the female intellect has any truth in it, it might be expected to be rather the other way, and that wives would, as a rule, be only too ready to adopt their husbands' opinions. In any case, contact has an undoubted tendency to produce unanimity, and the chances are therefore in favour of agreement. And that there should be intelligent agreement, a community of thought and feeling, on all matters of importance, is surely the first necessity for the healthy and harmonious development of family life. M. Simon has

drawn a vivid picture of the influence on
children of discordance between fathers
and mothers, even when there is nothing
like an open rupture.

'Cette femme qu'une religieuse a formée
et cet homme nourri des doctrines de
tolérance, peut-être d'indifférence, mariés
ensemble, sont un vivant anachronisme.
La femme est du dix-septième siècle et
l'homme de la fin du dix-huitième. Admet-
tons qu'ils vivent en bonne intelligence,
elle le croyant damné, lui la jugeant fana-
tique. Qu'arrivera-t-il, quand à leur tour,
ils enseigneront ? Et ils enseigneront ;
être père, être mère, c'est enseigner. La
mère répétera sa doctrine, puisée au cou-
vent ; le père, par prudence, se taira. Se
taira-t-il ? Si même il prend cela sur lui,

son silence sera commenté par ses actes.
Et que pensera l'enfant de cette contradiction, aussitôt qu'il pensera ? Il condam-
nera l'un ou l'autre, peut-être l'un et
l'autre.   Plus il aura l'esprit puissant, plus
vite il perdra respect. . . . Il semble à des
esprits sans portée que l'indifférence et la
foi vivront bien ensemble, parce que l'une
exige et l'autre céde ; mais céder à une
croyance sans l'accepter, c'est ne pas être.
La paix entre deux âmes est possible
quand elle est fondée sur l'identité de foi ;
elle est encore possible quand elle est
fondée sur le respect réciproque d'une foi
diverse et sincère ; mais appeler paix cette
absence de lutte qui naît de l'indifférence,
c'est confondre la paix avec la défaite et la
vie avec le néant.'

The author of 'Vincenzo' has given in
that remarkable story a view too painfully
lifelike to be disbelieved, of the conjugal
misery resulting from a profound disson-
ance between a husband and wife on religious and political questions, and asserts
that the wreck of domestic happiness so
graphically pictured represents a reality
far from uncommon. 'Would to God,'
he exclaims, 'that the case were an isolated one! But no; there is scarcely any
corner in Italy, scarcely any corner in
Europe, that does not exhibit plenty of
such and worse.' Such a state of things
could scarcely exist in England. The
counteracting influences are too many and
too strong. But it cannot be said that we
are exempt from danger. In how many

English families wives and sisters are clinging blindly to traditional beliefs and observances, from which husbands and brothers are turning away with indifference or dislike. How natural the transition from the theory which assigns ' to the one the supremacy of the head, to the other that of the heart'—to that further division which attributes to the one Reason, to the other Faith. Heartless Rationalism and imbecile credulity ! Is it in the union of these feeble and jarring tones that we shall find the full chord of family harmony ? Ought we not rather to turn with suspicion from these artificial attempts to apportion attributes and duties ? May we not welcome, as at least a step in the right direction, a change in our conventional habits, which may extend, though in ever so small a degree, the region of common thoughts and aims, common hopes and disappointments, common joys and common sorrows?

CHAPTER VI.

SPECIFIC SUGGESTIONS.

IF it be admitted that the law of human duty is the same for both sexes, and if the specific functions belonging to each demand substantially the same qualities for their performance, it appears to follow that the education required is likely to be, in its broader and more essential features, the same. What that education

ought to be has lately been much discussed, but at present without much sign
of approaching unanimity. That there
should be great difference of opinion is
natural, inasmuch as almost every one
is inclined to recommend for universal
adoption just what he happens to like
best himself; while, on the other hand,
a few people of a different turn of mind
are disposed to undervalue what they
possess themselves, and to give extra
credit to subjects or methods, the in-
sufficiency of which has not been brought
home to them by personal experience.
In the education of girls the selection
of subjects seems to be directed by no
principle whatever. Strong protests are
raised against assimilating it to that of

boys; but very little is said as to the particulars in which it ought to differ. The present distribution is, indeed, somewhat whimsical.   Inasmuch as young men go into offices where they have to conduct foreign correspondence, and, as they travel about all over the world, they are taught the dead languages.   As woman's place is the domestic hearth, and as middle class women rarely see a foreigner, they are taught modern languages with a special view to facility in speaking.   As men are supposed to work with their heads all day, and have nothing in the world to do when they are indisposed for reading but to smoke or to go to sleep, they are taught neither music nor drawing.   As women have always the resource of needlework, they learn music and drawing besides. As women are not expected to take part in political affairs, they are taught history. As men do, boys learn mathematics instead. In physical science, astronomy and botany are considered the ladies' department. Chemistry and mechanics being the branches most directly applicable to domestic uses, are reserved for boys.

These distinctions ought rather, however, to be spoken of as a thing of the past. The educators of boys and girls respectively are learning and borrowing from each other.* An approximation is

* With equal need, if what Lord Russell says is true :—' As it is at present, there is no doubt that women of the higher ranks have much more knowledge and information when their education is finished

already in progress, in which the encroachment, if it be an encroachment, is chiefly from the side of boys; for while Latin and mathematics are slowly making their way into girls' schools, we find that in the University local examinations, music, drawing, and modern languages have from the beginning been recognised as desirable for boys. It is,

than men have. But I cannot see any reason why our young men should not, while they have the advantage of public schools, at the same time be able to do a sum in the rule of three, and make themselves masters of the fact that James I. was not the son of Queen Elizabeth.'

In another place he says:—'It is to a dogged application to the Latin grammar perhaps that the precision of men, when compared to women, in this country is in great part to be attributed.'—*Earl Russell on the English Government and Constitution*, pp. 210, 208.

like most other things, very much a question of degree. The system of mutual isolation has never been thoroughly carried out. Even those who hold most strongly that classics and mathematics are proper for boys, and modern languages and the fine arts for girls, leave as common ground the wide field of English literature, in itself almost an education. To a large extent men and women read the same books, magazines, and newspapers; and though in the highest class of literature, written by scholars for scholars, and, therefore, full of classical and scientific allusions, there is much that women only half understand, the deficiency under which they labour is shared by many male readers.

Probably, after all, it matters less what is nominally taught, than that, whatever it is, it should be taught in the best way. Any subject may be made flat and unprofitable if unintelligently taught ; and, on the other hand, there is scarcely anything which may not be made an instrument of intellectual discipline, if wisely used. Then, again, all branches of knowledge are so closely connected and mutually dependent, that it is scarcely possible to learn anything which will not be found more or less useful hereafter in learning something else.   Even the much despised and denounced 'smattering of many things,' has its merits in this way, as well as in giving a certain breadth of vision, by opening vistas into innumerable fields of knowledge, never to be explored by any single human being. The degree in which the study of certain subjects cultivates certain faculties is a matter on which we are far from agreeing. Nor is it decided—in fact we have scarcely begun to discuss—what faculties most need cultivation. In the middle classes the imagination seems to be the one in which the deficiency is most marked. Every now and then some one recommends mathematics for girls as a curb to the imagination. It might be as well first to ascertain whether the imaginations of commonplace girls want to be curbed; whether, on the contrary, they do not want rather to be awakened and set to work, with something to work upon. The business of the imagination is not merely to build castles in the air, though that is, no doubt, a useful and commendable exercise; it has other and most important duties to perform. For, manifestly, an unimaginative person is destitute of one of the main elements of sympathy. Probably, if the truth were known, it would be found that injustice and unkindness are comparatively seldom caused by harshness of disposition. They are the result of an incapacity for imagining ourselves to be somebody else. Any one who has tried it must be aware of the enormous difficulty of conceiving the state of mind of a pauper or a thief. The same difficulty is experienced in a degree by any one in easy circumstances in realising the condition and looking from the point of view of a very poor, or comparatively poor person. It is probably equally difficult to ordinary minds to imagine the condition of always having more money than you quite know what to do with. The absence of sympathy between youth and age is traceable to the same want. Old people have either forgotten their own youth, or they remember it too well, and fall into the not less fatal mistake of supposing that the new youth is like their own. Young people, on their part, are equally at a loss to understand what it is to be old. In all the relations of life, the want of imagination produces defective sympathy, and defective sympathy brings in its train all sorts of vague and intolerable evils. In every branch of study a vivid imagination is a most powerful agent, aiding the memory, and bringing clearly before the mind the materials on which a judgment has to be formed.

This, however, is not the place to discuss the comparative importance of the mental faculties. Without going into the details of what, or how to teach, it will be more to the purpose to inquire whether there are any general measures, the working of which is likely to be beneficial, let the subjects and the methods of instruction be what they may.

Among the most necessary, and the most easily and immediately applicable, is the extension to women of such examinations as demand a high standard of attainment. The test of a searching examination is indispensable as a guarantee for the qualifications of teachers; it is wanted as a stimulus by young women studying with no immediate object in view, and no incentive to exertion other than the high, but dim and distant, purpose of self-culture. This purpose, regarded in its bearing on the general welfare, is indeed honourable and animating, and every other must be subordinate to it. But we must not forget that we have to deal with human and very imperfect beings; and it is not difficult to believe that young women of only average energy and perseverance, while working in the main towards the higher end, may yet need an occasionally recurring stage within sight, as an allurement to draw them on, and to help them in their struggle with the temptations to indolence which lie thick about their path. The fact of having an examination to work for, would not only be a stimulus to themselves, it would also serve as a defence against idle companions, whose solicitations it is hard to refuse on the mere ground of an abstract love of learning.

The want of examinations for women is not a new discovery. So long ago as 1841, Dr Arnold wrote to Mr Justice Coleridge :—'I feel quite as strongly as you do the extreme difficulty of giving to girls what really deserves the name of education intellectually. When —— was young, I used to teach her some Latin with her brothers, and that has been, I think, of real use to her, and she feels it now in reading and translating German, of which she does a great deal. But there is nothing for girls like the Degree examination, which concentrates one's reading so beautifully, and makes one master a certain number of books perfectly. And unless we had a domestic examination for young ladies, to be passed before they come out, and another, like the great go, before they come of age, I do not see how the thing can ever be effected. Seriously, I do not see how we can supply sufficient encouragement for systematic and laborious reading, or how we can insure many things being retained at once fully in the mind, when we are wholly without the machinery which we have for our boys.'

In another letter, speaking of the need of continual questioning in the case of a boy, he says, 'He wants this, and he wants it daily, not only to interest and excite him, but to dispel what is very apt to grow around a lonely reader not constantly questioned—a haze of indistinctness as to a consciousness of his own knowledge or ignorance ; he takes a vague impression for a definite one, an imperfect notion for one that is full and complete, and in this way he is continually deceiving himself.'

This is an exact description of the state

of the young female mind, even where there has been considerable cultivation. Women have 'general ideas,' which interest and occupy their minds, but produce little fruit, owing to their incompleteness and uncertainty. Of course, it would be absurd to recommend examinations as an infallible cure for this or any other mental defect. The familiar objections, that there are many things which no examination can test; that they sometimes encourage cram and check originality; and that, when abused, they foster ambition, and cause overexcitement and overwork—no doubt have some truth in them. But the question is whether, on the whole, examinations work for good or for evil; and the testimony of long experience seems to be strongly in

K

their favour. To refuse to test knowledge, because you cannot by the same process judge of moral excellence, is about as wise as to say that a man ought not to eat, because, unless he also takes exercise, he will not be in good health. Cram is no doubt a very bad thing, but it is not a necessary antecedent of examinations; and, after all, there are alternatives worse than cramming. It may be better even to cram than to leave the mind quite empty; and though the word has become, by perpetual reiteration, closely associated with the idea of examinations, it is as well to remember that it is quite possible for knowledge to be equally undigested, whether it has been got up for an examination or not. As to fostering ambition, the question seems to be, whether it is possible, or even desirable, entirely to eradicate it, and whether to direct it towards a respectable object, the pursuit of which at least implies some good moral qualities, may not be useful as diverting it from that meanest of aims—the only one held up indiscriminately to women of every grade—that of shining in society. The danger of injury to health, through excitement and overwork, is within the control of parents and teachers. As regards girls, the experience of the Cambridge local examinations has proved beyond a doubt that, where ordinary common sense is practised, there is no risk whatever of this sort.

There are at present no examinations

open to women of such standing as to constitute a fitting test of advanced scholarship. The examinations of the Society of Arts, being primarily intended for artisans, are manifestly inadequate; and the University local examinations are limited to students under eighteen. The University of London, having adopted the principle of making its examinations simply a test and standard of acquirement, without enforcing upon students that their knowledge should have been acquired by attendance at college lectures, or under any particular system, is in a peculiarly favourable position for giving assistance in this matter. The extension of the London examinations to women need present no greater difficulties than those which have been already overcome in throwing open the Cambridge local examinations to girls, and would go far towards supplying a want which every day becomes more pressing.

The access to progressive examinations, of such a character as to test and attest advanced attainments, would, there is every reason to believe, at once begin to work in lengthening the period of study. It would probably tell first upon the ladies' colleges; but its influence would not be limited to college students. Where circumstances make it inconvenient for a girl to attend classes, it may still be practicable for her to pursue her studies at home, so long as there is some definite and intelligible object in view. An essential requisite is the use of a room where she can be secure from trivial interruptions. This might seem obvious enough ; but those who know anything of family life in the middle class are aware that it is a privilege rarely accorded to young women. The best teaching within reach would, of course, be a great assistance, but would not be in all cases indispensable.

An increase in the number of colleges and a higher standard of efficiency would be the natural result of retaining the students under instruction for a longer time, and this again would improve the quality of teachers. Probably something more would still be required in the way of training for teachers. It seems to be the opinion of the persons best qualified to judge, that some technical instruction is required as a preparation for teaching, and that such instruction might be obtained by taking a short course at a training-college at the end of a general education.

The ladies' colleges may fairly be expected to supply 'the education of a lady.' The special training for any particular profession must be obtained in distinct schools. This, of course, applies to every branch of art. It applies also to the study of medicine. There is at present no medical school for women; and individual students are therefore obliged to obtain the necessary instruction privately. It is to be wished that one of the London hospitals, not connected with any existing medical school, should be reserved for female students and classes formed in connexion with it. If this were done, as it probably would be on the application of a sufficient number of students, the education of medical women would be provided for.

The preparation for business is, in most cases, simply a matter of arrangement, requiring nothing but the good will and hearty concurrence of the masters. The easiest thing would be for fathers to bring up their daughters to their own business; and, no doubt, this would often be done, if custom permitted. It is the fear of public opinion—of exciting astonishment and remark—that, probably more than any other cause, imposes upon parents what they feel to be a sort of moral and social obligation to keep their daughters idle.

In addition to other hindrances in the way of giving a thorough education to girls, there is one which presses heavily on persons of narrow incomes— namely, its costliness as compared with that of boys. This is a fact, notwithstanding the other fact, that the teachers of girls are, as a rule, much worse paid than the teachers of boys. It is traceable to two causes—the absence of endowments, and the smallness of girls' schools. Both these causes are removable.

With regard to endowments, there is reason to believe that a large proportion of those which are now appropriated to the use of boys were originally intended for both sexes. The founders do not seem to have known anything about the modern theories of separate education, and, when they established a school, had no idea of excluding any of ' the children ' of the parish or kin which it was designed to benefit. It is noticeable that, in cases where girls happen to be expressly mentioned in the foundation deeds, Latin and accounts are almost invariably named in the course of instruction laid down. There is much difference of opinion as to the permanent usefulness of endowments. Some people think they do more harm than good, and would like to get rid of them altogether. This seems a somewhat extreme view; and, at any rate, as the endowments exist, something must be done with them. If it is for the general good that education should be much more expensive, and, therefore, much more difficult to get, for a girl than for a boy; or if the balance is redressed by greater willingness on the part of parents to make sacrifices in behalf of their daughters, it may be well to let the present distribution stand. But it appears rather that the education of women is at present exactly at the stage at which artificial support is wanted. There are many ways in which it might be applied. Probably the most useful at the present juncture would be the foundation of exhibitions and scholarships, awarded under such varying conditions as to give them the widest possible range. Taking the middle classes generally, there seems to be no reason why they should not pay for the education of their children at cost price; but there are many exceptions, and the legitimate use of all eleemosynary aid seems to be to meet special cases of misfortune. For this reason it is desirable that, besides exhibitions and scholarships awarded after a competitive examination —which would act as an encouragement to industry and ability—there should be in the hands of governors and trustees a power of conferring free or assisted education without competition. Scholarships might be tenable at elementary schools, at a college, at a medical school, or at schools of art; or there might be exhibitions available for apprenticeship to any profession or trade whatsoever, at the discretion of the trustees.

In the meantime, without any aid from public sources, a good deal might be done by a more judicious use of existing means. The present mode of carrying on girls' schools involves an enormous waste of teaching power. Fifteen or twenty girls absorb a staff amply sufficient for three or four times the number. This is inevitable in small schools; and the consequence follows, that in many boarding-schools for girls the terms are considerably higher than at Rugby or Harrow. It is doubtful whether very large boarding-schools would work well; but the difficulty may be got over in another way, by establishing a thoroughly good day-school, and clustering round it boarding-houses of moderate size, according to the demand. In places like Blackheath, Clapham, St John's Wood, or in any locality where girls' schools congregate, this plan might be adopted, and would combine many of the respective advantages of large and small schools. The facilities for classification, companionship in study, healthy public spirit, and a general kind of open-airiness which go with large numbers, would be found in the school. The boardinghouses would have the quietness and something of the domestic character which it is difficult to get in a household conducted on a very large scale. The popularity of small boarding-schools is probably chiefly owing to their fancied resemblance to a home circle. There is an impression that a group of girls, all about the same age, and without father or brothers, constitute something like a family. It is really much more like a nunnery; and there is reason to believe that, in a less degree, just those evils which are said to attach to conventual life are rife in boardingschools.

A sense of these evils leads some people to prefer the system of private governesses. This no doubt has recommendation; it certainly has serious drawbacks. Among those which are inevitable is the effect of a lonely life on the governess. Without going into sentimental wailings over her unhappy lot, it must be confessed that her position is peculiarly isolated

She spends the greater part of her time in intercourse with young and immature minds, only varied by unequal association with the parents or grown-up brothers and sisters of her pupils. The society of her equals in age and position is entirely wanting, and the natural tendency of such mental solitude is to produce childishness, angularity, and narrow-mindedness. It must be a very strong character indeed which can do without the wholesome trituration and the expansive influence of equal companionship, and this is just what a governess cannot have. A great effort may be made to treat her as one of the family, but she does not really belong to the people, or even to their class. She is always a bird of passage, and in this respect her position is worse than that of a servant, who, besides having the companionship of fellowservants, may look forward to remaining in one family for life. A governess must always be prepared to leave when the term of temporary service expires, and this is in itself an obstacle to the formation of strong attachments. And if it is true that the conditions of governess life have a deteriorating effect on character, it follows that the pupils will in a degree more or less be losers. Whether there may be advantages or conveniences which more than compensate for what is lost, is a question which must be affected by considerations varying in individual cases. Similarly, with regard to boardingschools, a first-

L

rate mistress may be able to offer certain advantages attainable in no other way. The conclusion arrived at goes no farther than this, that, other things being equal, a large day-school attended by scholars living either at home or in small board-inghouses, has a clear advantage, both as regards economy and mental and moral training, over the rival systems of board-ingschools and private governesses. It follows that in any direct efforts which may be made for the improvement of elementary education, the foundation or strengthening of well conducted day-schools is the wisest course to adopt.

The foregoing suggestions must of course be subject to all sorts of modifica-tions, according to temporary and local necessities. Specific schemes, adapted to circumstances, will be devised as occasions arise. In the meantime, any kind of recognition of the fact that the education of women is a matter worth thinking about, is of the utmost practical value. In this point of view, as indicating and expressing a growing sense of the importance of the subject, the extension to girls of the local examinations of the Universities of Cambridge and Edinburgh, and the steps taken by the Schools Inquiry Commission in their pending investigations, have an indirect influence quite out of proportion to the immediate and calculable results obtained, affording a moral support and encouragement the effect of which it is not easy to estimate.

CHAPTER VII.

CONCLUSION.

TO guard against misconception on so obscure and so complex a subject as that of the present inquiry is a somewhat hopeless endeavour. But it may, perhaps, be worth while to say once more, what has so often been said already, that those who ask for a fuller and freer life for women have no desire to interfere with distinctions of sex.

The question under debate is not whether, as a matter of fact, there is such a thing as distinctive manhood and womanhood; for that no one denies. The dispute is rather as to the degree in which certain qualities, commonly regarded as respectively masculine and feminine characteristics, are such intrinsically, or only conventionally; and further, as to the degree of prominence which it is desirable to give to the specific differences in determining social arrangements. It is not against the recognition of real distinctions, but against arbitrary judgments, not based upon reason, that the protest is raised. If, in the exigencies of controversy, expressions may sometimes be used which seem to involve a denial of differences in the respective natures of women and of men, it must be regarded as a misfortune for which the advocates of restriction and suppression are responsible. When broad assertions are made as to natural fitness and unfitness, and a course of action is founded upon them, it becomes necessary, at least, to ask for proof. When proof is wanting, it is not unnatural to fall back upon feeling; and prejudices, dignified by the name of instincts, are appealed to as decisive when rational argument fails. The whole question is clouded over by this confusing procedure. The instincts, to which so much importance is attached, differ in the most bewildering manner. What one person's instinct pronounces lawful and becoming, another finds revolting. Assumptions are made, and a fabric of argument is built up upon data which are unverified, and which it is at present impossible either to verify or absolutely to contradict. For, until artificial appliances are removed, we cannot know anything certainly about the native distinctions. As to the future, who can say? It may be that,

> 'In the long years liker must they grow,
> The man be more of woman, she of man;
> He gain in sweetness and in moral height,
> Nor lose the wrestling thews that throw the world;
> She mental breadth, nor fail in childward care;
> More as the double-natured poet each:'

or it may be that, when 'full-summed in all their powers,' new shades of unlikeness—refinements of diversity hitherto unimagined—may appear. It is neither necessary nor expedient to prejudge the question ; and those whose faith in the reality and permanence of the native distinctions is the strongest are the least tempted to make rash assertions on either side. The excessive apprehensiveness shown by some people on this point seems to indicate a deeprooted distrust in the strength of their position. The fear betrays a doubt. No one urges that girls should be denied the use of cold water, or fresh air, or light, or animal food, lest they should grow into boys. Yet that these conditions tend to produce masculine vigour cannot be denied. Those who are afraid that a free range of thought and action would injure the delicacy of the female mind, ought, in consistency, to carry their precautions a little farther. The atmosphere of a hot-house, judiciously darkened, abstinence from exercise, and a vegetarian diet would have an evident tendency to pro-duce a sickly delicacy of complexion, to give languor to the limbs, and feebleness to the voice, and in every way to make girls much more unlike their brothers than they were by nature. And if this is the object of education, the appro-priate means ought to be used.

In the meantime, a great part of the difficulties which beset every question concerning women would be at once re-moved by a frank recognition of the fact, that there is between the sexes a deep and broad basis of likeness. The hypothesis that men and women are essentially and radically different, embarrasses every discussion. When facts are proved and admitted, scarcely any progress has been made, because it is assumed that their action is modified by their application to the feminine nature. Conditions which would certainly make a man happy or miserable, as the case might be, are supposed to have a different, if not an exactly opposite, effect upon a woman. The theory has been asserted and re-asserted so incessantly, that even women themselves have been partly persuaded to believe it. And it is, no doubt, so far true, that while the education and the circumstances of women are widely different from those of men, every agency brought to bear upon either must act somewhat differently. But to create facts, and then to argue from them as if they were the result of an unalterable destiny, is a method which convinces only so long as it is enforced by prejudice. 'Chacun selon sa capacité'—'à chaque producteur l'ouvrage auquel il est propre'—these are maxims of unquestioned validity. But who shall say for another—much more, who shall say for half the human race —this, or this, is the measure of your capacity; this, and no other, is the work you are qualified to perform? 'Women's work,' it is said, 'is helping work.' Certainly it is. And is it men's work to hinder? The vague information that women are to be ministering angels is no answer to the practical questions, Whom are they to help, and how? The easy solution, that it is their nature to do what men cannot do, or cannot do so well, has never been adopted in practice, inasmuch as everything in the world that there is to do, the care of infants alone excepted, men are doing; and there is nothing that a trained man cannot do better than an untrained woman. Literature and art, teaching, nursing, cooking, sewing—these are the recognised feminine occupations, and they are all shared by men. The pursuit of them does not turn men into women, or women into men. Miss Yonge and Mrs Oliphant 'help' Mr Trollope in supplying the world with novels ; and it is not thought necessary to guard either party from writing masculine or feminine novels respectively. Schoolmasters and schoolmistresses do not come into unseemly rivalry, although women teach boys and men teach girls. By and by it will be found equally superfluous to prescribe limitations in any department of thought or industry.

It can scarcely be necessary to discuss at length the difficulty expressed in the frequent question,—if women take to doing men's work, what are men to do? Will not the intrusion of women into professions and trades already overcrowded, lower the current rate of wages, and by thus making men less able to support their families—in the long run, do more harm than good? As to the manner and degree in which the labour-market might be affected by such a readjustment as is proposed, it is difficult to predict anything with certainty. It is impossible to tell beforehand how many women would take to what is called (by a very conspicuous *petitio principii*) men's work, and how large a portion of their lives they would devote to it. If women, already destined to work for their bread, chose to earn it in some hitherto unaccustomed way, it is obvious that in the exact measure in which their entrance into a new profession reduced the rate of wages in that particular calling, it would tend to raise it in some other which they would have otherwise pursued, and the balance would thus be redressed. If, on the other hand, women are not supporting themselves, they are being supported by somebody else, consuming either present earnings or accumulated savings. To keep them from earning money does not prevent their spending it. Let us suppose the event, not a very probable one, that the introduction of women into the medical profession would lower the average rate of remuneration by one-third, in which case the professional income of an ordinary medical man would be lessened in the same proportion. Let us suppose, also —a not at all improbable case—that the doctor's wife, or sister, or daughter, would earn, in the practice of *her* pro-

fession, a sum equivalent to the one-
third he has lost. Evidently, the doctor
and his family would be where they
were, neither better nor worse off than
before. In the meantime, the public
would be so much the richer by getting
its medical attendance one-third cheaper.
Whatever might be the temporary effect
of opening any particular profession to
women, one thing is certain, it can never
be for the interest of society, in a purely
economical aspect, to keep any class of
its members in idleness. A man who
should carry one of his arms in a sling,
in order to secure greater efficiency and
importance to the other, would be regarded as a lunatic. The one free mem-
ber might very probably gain a little

extra dexterity, of an abnormal sort, but that the man would be on the whole a loser, is obvious. The case of the body politic is precisely analogous. The economical argument is all in favour of setting everybody to work. Such difficulties as exist are of a moral or æsthetic nature, and require for their disentanglement considerations of a different sort from those which govern the comparatively easy economical question.

Much misapprehension has probably arisen from a confusion between a standard or law of life and the persons to whom it is applied. A standard or law says nothing about the character of the persons who are expected to conform to it. It pronounces no opinion upon

M

their nature beyond what is implied in assuming it to be not impossible for them to live by it. The command, 'Thou shalt love the Lord thy God with all thy heart, and thy neighbour as thyself,' implies that such love is possible to men; but it may be manifested in countless ways—in heroic conflict or in patient endurance, in passionate ardour or meek submission. If it be true that certain gifts and graces are specially congenial to the masculine or feminine nature, the presentation of a common standard will draw them out according to their kind, without the risk of seeming to dispense with the less easy virtues. Just as when you plant two rose-trees in the same ground, you imply the belief that certain general conditions of soil and atmosphere are good for both, but you make no attempt to influence variations of colour or of perfume; so the Christian theory of education implies an essential resemblance between the sexes, without interfering in any way with native differences. If, indeed, you adopt the analogy, not without a certain fanciful charm, according to which men are trees and women flowers, the separate system is right. You do wisely to plant the oak in the forest, and to shelter the delicate geranium in the hothouse. But this view implies that men and women are of a different genus, which no one in his senses would maintain. The popular simile of the oak and the ivy is equally untenable. Advocates on both sides are apt to talk as if men and women were distinct races, handing down their respective characteristics from generation to generation. The fact is, as every one knows, that hereditary qualities are transmitted from father to daughter, and from mother to son, with much impartiality. The influences tending to create dissimilarity, which, in our day at least, are at work, without a moment's intermission, from the cradle to the grave, are incessantly neutralised in each successive generation. If it were not so, it is difficult to imagine what the human race would become. One thing is certain, it would very soon cease to be human.

Writers on this subject commonly adopt

somewhat of a threatening tone in reference to any proposed change. They warn
women that if the oak and ivy theory is
given up, what is called the old chivalry
will die out, and they must no longer
expect to be protected. And it is further
urged that men would suffer, no less than
women, from the absence of any demand
upon their protective instincts. We are
indebted to Mr Kingsley for a very clear
and moderate statement of this view in a
chapter of ' The Roman and the Teuton '
on the Lombard Laws.

' It is to be remarked,' he says, ' that
no free woman can live in Lombardy, or,
I believe, in any Teutonic state, save
under the " mundium " of some one. You
should understand this word " mund."

Among most of the Teutonic races, women, slaves and youths, at least not of age to carry arms, were under the mund of some one. Of course, primarily the father, head of the family, and if he died, an uncle, elder brother, &c. The married woman was, of course, under the mund of her husband. He was answerable for the good conduct of all under his mund; he had to pay their fines if they offended; and he was bound, on the other hand, to protect them by all lawful means.

'This system still lingers in the legal status of women in England, for good and evil; the husband is more or less answerable for the wife's debts; the wife, till lately, was unable to gain property apart from her husband's control; the wife is supposed, in certain cases of law, to act under the husband's compulsion. All these, and many others, are relics of the old system of mund for women; and that system has, I verily believe, succeeded. It has called out, as no other system could have done, chivalry in the man. It has made him feel it a duty and an honour to protect the physically weaker sex. It has made the woman feel that her influence, whether in the state or in the family, is to be not physical and legal, but moral and spiritual; and that it therefore rests on a ground really nobler and deeper than that of the man. The modern experiments for emancipating women from all mund, and placing them on a physical and legal equality with the man, may be right, and may be ultimately successful. We must not hastily prejudge them. But of this we may be almost certain, that, if they succeed, they will cause a widespread revolution in society, of which the patent danger will be, the destruction of the feeling of chivalry, and the consequent brutalisation of the male sex.'

These are terrible warnings, and may well make any one hesitate in lifting a finger to aid in a revolution charged with such disastrous possibilities. But is it really true that the male sex is likely to be brutalised by learning that a man must no longer rely upon physical and legal influence, but must rest his claims to allegiance on a moral and spiritual basis? Is it good for a man to feel that his influence rests on a ground less noble and deep than that of women, and to satisfy himself with a lower moral position? The mund system may have succeeded,—in other words, it may have been the best thing possible, in a rude and barbarous age, when serfdom also was in full force and 'succeeded' in its way—a time when force was met by force, and individual protection was a surer resource than that of law. But even as applying to those days, the success of the system seems to have been somewhat incomplete. How it worked— or failed to work—Mr Kingsley shows in a few graphic lines, in his recent tale, 'Hereward.' Describing the fate of the little Torfrida, his hero's daughter, he tells us, that 'she was married to Hugh of Evermue, who is not said to have kicked her; and was, according to them of Crowland, a good friend to their monastery, and therefore, doubtless, a good man. Once, says wicked report, he offered to strike her, as was the fashion in those chivalrous days. Whereon she turned upon him like a tigress, and bidding him remember that she was the daughter of Hereward and Torfrida, gave him such a beating, that he, not wishing to draw sword upon her, surrendered at discretion; and they lived all their lives afterwards as happily as most other people in those times.'

Mr Gladstone lays down, that 'as the law of force is the law of the brute creation, so in proportion as he is under the yoke of that law does man approximate to the brute; and in proportion, on the other hand, as he has escaped from its dominion, is he ascending into the higher sphere of being and claiming relationship with Deity. But the emancipation and due ascendancy of women are not a mere fact: they are the emphatic assertion of a principle; and that principle is the dethronement of the law of force, and the enthronement of other and higher laws in its place, and in its despite.' The advocates of the protective theory seem scarcely to have realised that the idea of protection implies the corresponding idea of attack. It assumes, as part of its essence, that somebody is attacking, or what occasion would there be for defence?

Might it not be well for everybody to abandon the attitude of attack? To assert that in a civilised country women want such protection as any human arm can give, is a contradiction in terms. It is supposing, either that the law permits outrages upon the defenceless, or that it can be broken with impunity. That we in England are as yet only partially emerged from barbarism is indeed true. The time-honoured customs handed down from the days of Hugh of Evermue have not yet disappeared, and cases of assault, almost invariably committed by the natural protector, are not uncommon in English households. But the law undertakes to interfere — and does interfere, though as yet in a somewhat impotent

manner—for the defence of hapless wives
and children. It can scarcely be the true
policy of an age which professes to be
enlightened and humane, to suffer general
licence to prevail, in order that a few rare
souls, able to be a law to themselves and
other people, may have the occasion for
displaying exceptional heroism. If the
scheme of Divine Providence requires
that there should be outlets for the protective energies, they are likely to be
found for a long time yet, in the infir-
mities of age, of infancy, and of poverty,
without encouraging morbid or affected
weakness in human beings intended by
nature to be healthy and strong. There
is still plenty of fighting to do, though
the progress of civilisation has removed

the warfare into new fields, and demands new weapons. Evil now appears in a subtle, intangible shape, against which physical strength is of little avail. But the generosity and the courage which constituted the true beauty and worth of chivalry can never become obsolete. The chivalrous spirit now shows itself in the abandonment of unjust privileges, in the enactment of equal laws, and in facing ridicule, opposition, and discouragement in behalf of unpopular ideas. The great battle between good and evil is for ever going on. The form is renewed from age to age, but the spirit is the same. Let us take care lest, in clinging to forms from which the spirit has departed, in shutting our eyes to keep out the dawning day, we may be blindly fighting the battle of the Philistines, all unwittingly ranged among the enemies of the cause we desire to serve.

BALLANTYNE, ROBERTS, AND COMPANY, PRINTERS, EDINBURGH.